We'll Always Be There For You

Library of Congress Control Number: 2007001020

ISBN 978-1-59566-488-4

Written by Annette Aubrey
Edited by Sarah Medina
Designed by Alix Wood
Illustrated by Patrice Barton
Consultancy by David Hart

Publisher Steve Evans
Creative Director Zeta Davies
Senior Editor Hannah Ray

Printed and bound in China

We'll Always Be There For You

Annette Aubrey

Illustrated by
Patrice Barton

QEB Publishing

QEB

Jonathan Harrison Spencer
was having a very **Sad** day.
His mom and his dad had just told him
that Daddy was **going away**.

It was very soon after breakfast
when Jonathan's mommy did say,
"Come, Jonathan, and sit with us.
There's something we need to explain."

Jon, Daddy and I both love you.
You're the most special boy that we know.
But we haven't been getting along lately
and we've both agreed Daddy will go.

Jonathan could not believe it!
It was all such a shock and a fright.
"**Mom! Dad!** Please say that **you're sorry**
and things will be better tonight."

Then Jonathan started to worry. "Dad, what will Mom and I do, living at home, just the two of us? And what will happen to you?

"Where are you going to live, Dad?
Will you stay in a house that is new?"

With tears in his eyes, Jonathan cried,
"Dad, what will we do without you?"

Jonathan thought a hundred thoughts.
He felt them all spin in his head.

"Are my mommy and daddy breaking up because of something I might have said?

"Or maybe I did something terrible,
so Dad wants a new home instead?
Perhaps Mom and Dad both hate it
when I'm naughty and won't go to bed."

Jonathan Harrison
Spencer
felt confused—and he
also felt **mad**.

His tummy was knotted
and achy,
and his heart was empty
and sad.

He felt that he needed a cuddle from his mom, and then from his dad because this was the very hardest day that young Jon had ever had.

Jonathan's parents came close by him.
They sat quietly by his side.
They took him gently into their arms
and held him while he cried.

We are sorry that we have hurt you. Jon, we're sorry we've made you sad. What you are feeling is very natural, but you will not always feel this bad.

You might not understand this.
You may not believe what we say.
But we promise you, our darling son,
you will not **always**

feel this way.

And although we may be parting,
we will always look after you.
We will forever love and protect you
in **Mom's,** and in **Dad's home,** too.

"You really did nothing to cause this."
Mom softly wiped Jonathan's tears.
"Children do not cause such problems!
Of this, we are both very clear."

Dad said, We will find the way forward
that works best for all three of us here.
We adults will solve the **big** problems
and you needn't have any fears.

"Remember, we're always here for you.
We have loved you since time began.
We will listen to whatever you want to say
and we will help you however we can.

"And of all the things we tell you, dear, you must try to remember this one:

We will always be your parents and you will always be our son."

Jonathan felt a little better
than he did at the start of the day.
It was good to hear all the different things
that his mom and his dad had to say.

He was glad that he could ask questions.
He felt better and safer that way.
Now he knew they could still be a family
in the future, as well as today.

NOTES FOR PARENTS AND TEACHERS

- Look at the front cover of the book together. Talk about the picture. Can your children guess what the book is going to be about?

- On pages 4—6, Jonathan finds out that his dad is "going away." Ask your children what they think that means.

- On page 7, we start to read about Jonathan's feelings. Ask your children what they think Jonathan feels when he finds out that his dad is moving out. Why do they think that Jonathan asks his mom and dad to say sorry to each other? Explain that, even though children may want to help to sort things out, this is really a job for the grown-ups.

- On pages 8—9, Jonathan worries about what will happen to everyone when his dad leaves. Ask your children what they think Jonathan is feeling now, and what the hardest part of this is for him. What do they think Jonathan needs most right now?

- On pages 10—11, Jonathan wonders if his mom and dad are breaking up because of something he said or did. This is a common worry for children whose parents are separating. Say clearly to your children that adults' problems can never be caused by children.

- On pages 12—14, Jonathan experiences many different feelings. His parents understand this and comfort him. Ask your children how they think Jonathan feels when his mom and dad hold him in their arms while he cries? How do they think this helps him?

- Sometimes, adults' problems have a big impact on children. On page 15, Jonathan's parents acknowledge this and apologize to him. Discuss this with your children. Do they think this makes Jonathan feel better?

- On pages 16—17, Jonathan's parents reassure him that, even though they may be parting, they will continue to take care of him, love him, and protect him. Ask your children how they think Jonathan feels when his parents say these things. Do they think that he feels safer or relieved?

- On page 18, Jonathan's mom reassures him that he did nothing to cause his dad to leave. Remind your children that children can never cause their parents to separate.

- On page 19, Jonathan's dad tells Jonathan that he has no need to be fearful about the future. He says that he and Jonathan's mom will find solutions that work for all three of them. Ask your children if they think this is reassuring for Jonathan.

- On page 20, Jonathan's parents say that they will listen to him and try to help him. Ask your children how they think this makes Jonathan feel.

- Sometimes, a child needs to hear that it is OK to continue to love both his parents (and not take sides) and that both of his parents will continue to love him, too. Look at page 21. Ask your children if they think that Jonathan feels that both of his parents still love him. Do the children think that Jonathan feels it's OK to still love his dad as much as he always has, even though his dad is leaving?

- On page 23, Jonathan realizes that he and his parents will still be a family. Ask your children how they think this makes Jonathan feel. Ask if people can still be in your family even if they do not live with you. Discuss what families are like. Ask who belongs in your children's families. Ask them to name all the people who belong in their families, even if they do not live with them.